DOCTOR WHO
THE COMPANIONS

JOHN NATHAN-TURNER
ILLUSTRATED BY STUART HUGHES

By arrangement with BBC Publications
a division of BBC Enterprises Ltd.

Piccadilly Press · London

To Kath and Sam
with love always

Phototypeset by Area Graphics Ltd, Letchworth, Herts
Printed in Hong Kong by South Sea International Press Ltd
for the publisher Piccadilly Press Ltd, 1986
15 Golders Green Crescent, London NW11 8LA

Designed by Cherriwyn Magill

British Library Cataloguing in Publication Data

Nathan -Turner, John
Dr. Who: the companions.
1. Doctor Who (Television programme)
I. Title   II. Hughes, Stuart
791.45′72   PN1992.77.D6/

ISBN 0-946826-29-3 Paperback
0-946826-62-5 Hardback

John Nathan-Turner divides his time between houses in London and
Brighton. He is the longest-standing producer of *Doctor Who*,
and his main passion is the theatre.

Stuart Hughes lives in London. He has been a freelance illustrator
for a number of years. A lot of his work has been for science-
fiction, and computer books. All his commissions are used to
help finance the house he is renovating.

Stuart Hughes would like to thank
Dominic and Val for all their help.

The author wishes to thank Christopher H. Bidmead and Johnny Byrne
for their cooperation.

CONTENTS

INTRODUCTION

It used to be claimed that there were just two requirements to be a 'companion' in *Doctor Who*, the world's longest-running science-fiction TV series.

(1) To be able to scream and run at the same time!

(2) To be able to say 'What do we do next, Doctor?' with conviction!!

Before you pick up your pen to apply for a job, let us consider the above seriously. Although, particularly in the early days of *Doctor Who*, the above could be unkindly said to be virtually all the companions did, this is not so, or is it?

The primary function of a companion is to provide the Doctor with someone to talk to, someone to confide in, someone to protect. In terms of audience-identification, the companion's role is vitally important. Whether the companion is from another planet or good old Earth, the younger viewers relate to him or her. The companion represents the younger viewer and he/she hopefully asks the questions that all viewers would like to ask. (The Doctor is so vastly intelligent that someone is required to ask for an answer in plain English, rather than high-powered technical jargon.)

To avoid repetition of the Doctor's interference in galactic affairs, quite often the companion is the reason the Doctor visits certain places – for example, Tegan's requests to get to Heathrow Airport resulted in many an interesting escapade. These and other requests prevent the inevitable criticism of the Doctor's 'aimless wanderings.'

Sometimes a companion may land him or herself in trouble and consequently the Doc gets embroiled in a new situation. In other words the companion is an enormously useful plot-device.

With the advent of Sarah Jane Smith, so brilliantly played by Elisabeth Sladen, companions took on a much more rounded existence. In 1973 when Sarah Jane first appeared, women's liberation was much in evidence, and here was a companion who answered the Doctor back. Although Sarah Jane cared desperately for the Doctor, she had much more confidence in herself than previous companions. Of course this often resulted in trouble for the Doctor and herself, but Sarah Jane proved to be a leading character in her own right.

However, one of the problems I discovered later with companions of my own devising was that the more rounded the character, the more it required development. And development of character takes air-time and this reduces the amount of dramatisation air-time and before you know where you are, a science-fiction adventure series is taking on a soap-opera flavour. So, slowly but surely, writers and script editors *and* producers decide to play down the character development of the companion (in any case after twenty-three years we know comparatively little about the Doctor) and concentrate on the drama of the story.

If you're not careful, before you know where you are, after a fascinating introduction to a new companion, he or she is reduced to someone who says 'What do we do next, Doctor?' and runs and screams extremely well. But is this so?...

Inevitably, I have concentrated on the companions with which I have worked, and those which I have devised.

ADRIC

Played by Matthew Waterhouse
First Appearance: *Full Circle*   25th October 1980
Last Re-appearance: *The Caves of Androzani*   16th March 1984

Adric was the first new companion to be introduced after I took over as producer of *Doctor Who* in November 1979. The character first appeared in my third story at the helm, *Full Circle*.

Full Circle was actually written by a founder-member of the Doctor Who Appreciation Society. Christopher H. Bidmead, my script editor, had been going through the files and discovered a wealth of material accumulated over the years from a young man called Andrew Smith. Previous script editors and producers had written encouraging notes on the file about his storylines and scripts and Christopher was keen to encourage him further. Andrew was then eighteen years old and Chris spent a great deal of time with him converting an idea called *The Planet that Slept* into *Full Circle*. I know Andrew would agree that Chris was generous with his time and talent and he and Andrew came up with a super script.

The character of Adric was almost totally of Chris's devising; even the name Adric (an anagram of scientist Dirac) was his idea. I had suggested a character who was a cross between the Artful Dodger and Oliver Twist, and Chris came up with the following:

Adric

Adric is fifteen, small for his age, wiry and strong, with short, straight, black hair. His dominating elder brother, Varsh, was the leader of a juvenile street gang on the planet Alzarius – and under his tuition Adric learned to lie and steal, activities which are the dark side of his natural optimistic brashness and enormous intellectual curiosity.
Adric never fitted into the gang he was pressed into by his brother, partly because of his superior education, and partly because he is a born non-conformist, even among outlaws. When he met the Doctor his strong sense of self-preservation prompted him to assume an air of subdued innocence and false naivety. Though a disguise, this impersonation reminds us of Adric's very real vulnerability as a mortal (as opposed to the Time Lords).

6

With the last of his family ties broken, Adric stowed away in the Tardis. The Doctor wanted to return Adric to Alzarius, but what with one thing and another . . . Meanwhile, Adric's true character is emerging – enquiring, intelligent, but definitely and irritatingly a mendacious magpie. The Doctor's view of his responsibility towards the boy shifts; rather than return him to a planet where he will resume life as a criminal, wouldn't a certain amount of education, reform, and expansion of his moral horizon be appropriate. . .?

I hope Matthew Waterhouse won't mind me telling the following story, but when I was auditioning potential Adrics, I was looking for a young actor who was not the type to be found on the front of chocolate boxes! Having chosen Matthew as the best possible candidate for the part, despite his lack of experience, I was pleased that his complexion was not clear. This seemed to me to totally fit the bill for a young roughneck.

Television cameras nearly always add one stone to the real weight of the performer, and some performers look better on TV and others look much better in the flesh. No-one is totally able to explain this – it's just something that happens. Well, the TV cameras loved Matthew – he looked so much more striking than I wanted. I summoned the make-up designer to my office in the studio and asked why she'd covered up all his natural blemishes. She informed me that Matthew was only wearing a light dusting of powder to stop his face from shining. I went onto the studio floor to see for myself and she was telling the truth! The cameras loved him!

I remember too that for some of Matthew's initial episodes, he wore a hairpiece. I wanted Adric to have long hair and Matthew's previous job on a BBC classic serial had required him to have his hair cut short. So a hairpiece was made and fitted. During Adric's first filming session, the character had to swim in a lake and everyone, especially the make-up designer, held their breath as we filmed the swimming sequence, lest the hairpiece went sinking to the bottom. We didn't have a spare!

When it came to Adric's departure, I decided to go for broke. I asked Eric Saward, who was writing the script *Earthshock* to kill off the character of Adric in as emotional a way as possible. Adric was to be the first *long-running* companion to be killed.

7

When Matthew in due course read the script, he refused to speak to me for almost two weeks.

During my discussions with the director of *Earthshock*, Peter Grimwade, I decided we should end the episode which ended with Adric's death without the traditional signature tune, and roll the credits over a black background with the broken badge of mathematical excellence which Adric always wore. I had remembered watching an episode of *Coronation Street* many years before, when the death of a character named Martha Longhurst in the snug of the Rovers Return had been followed by a silent list of credits. I also remembered the effect it had had on many people, especially myself. So I decided to use the same technique.

With a long-running science-fiction adventure series there comes a time when people take it for granted. They know deep down that the Doctor, the following week, will somehow extricate himself from the situation in which he is placed, even though they may be fascinated as to how he'll achieve it. I felt at this time that the audience needed a jolt and the death of one of its regular characters seemed an ideal way to achieve it.

On the night of the transmission of Adric's death, the BBC switchboard was jammed. Calls of protest, crying children, etc. The audience had been forced out of potential lethargy with regard to *Doctor Who*. The following day I received several calls from parents whose children were unable to distinguish between the character Adric and the actor Matthew and were inconsolable. It was fantastic that I was able to tell the worried parents that if their children watched *This is Your Life* that week, they could see, as Eamonn Andrews put it, 'a reconstituted Matthew Waterhouse'. (The subject of the programme was the current Doctor, Peter Davison.)

I think the impact of the death of Adric was so immense that Matthew now has no regrets as to the way he departed from the series.

BARBARA WRIGHT
Played by Jacqueline Hill
First Appearance: *An Unearthly Child*   23rd November 1963
Last Appearance: *The Chase*   26th June 1965

Jacqueline returned to *Doctor Who* briefly as Lexa in the story *Meglos*, during my first season as producer. She announced after the pressures of the first studio session, 'Nothing has changed. It's like coming home.' We made no mention in the script of Lexa's physical similarity to Barbara.

BEN

Played by Michael Craze

First Appearance: *The War Machines*   25th June 1966
Last Appearance: *The Faceless Ones*   13th May 1967

I was delighted in November 1985 when Michael, who has now returned to acting, joined us for the *Children in Need* appeal. An all-time record of £4,000,000 plus was raised.

THE BRIGADIER
(Brigadier Lethbridge-Stewart)

Played by Nicholas Courtney

First Appearance as the Brigadier: *The Invasion*   2nd November 1968
Last Appearance: *The Five Doctors*   25th November 1983

There has always been much discussion as to the status of The Brigadier. Should the character be regarded as a companion or not? My personal opinion is that undoubtedly he should, although my own list of companions does not include Captain Yates or Sergeant Benton. Had the Brigadier not reappeared after *Terror of the Zygons* with Doctor Number Four, maybe I would feel differently.

Let us examine how his reappearances occurred. In preparation for the twentieth season of the series, Eric Saward and I had commissioned Peter Grimwade to write Turlough's first story – *Mawdryn Undead*. I seem to recall it was Peter who first mentioned his need of a male character from the Doctor's past. Because the setting for the story was an English public school, the character of Ian Chesterton, one of the original Doctor's first three travelling companions and a schoolteacher to boot, was ideal. Unfortunately William Russell, who played Ian in the series, was unavailable. (When I took over as producer I introduced a three-year ban after an actor/actress had appeared recognisably in the series. I understand that prior to this, a two-year ban was in operation.) So our next call was to the agent of Ian Marter (Harry Sullivan) but Ian was engaged on working in a soap-opera in New Zealand and wouldn't be available either. The Brigadier then sprang to mind and fortunately, Nicholas was both free and delighted at the prospect of returning.

It was while we were recording *Mawdryn Undead* that pieces of the jigsaw that were to become *The Five Doctors* Anniversary Special began to fall into place. Carole Ann Ford (Susan) had agreed to return to accompany the first Doctor, so brilliantly recreated by the late Richard Hurndall. Lis Sladen (Sarah Jane) had also agreed to take part, though at that time, I thought that she would accompany Tom Baker's Doctor (Tom Baker later withdrew from the project). Janet Fielding (Tegan) was under contract for the special too and I *mentally* had Katy Manning waiting in the wings to join Jon Pertwee's Doctor. It seemed to me that we needed another male companion in the programme, as the only one contracted was Mark Strickson (Turlough). I just couldn't see Turlough surrounded by an unending stream of ladies, though I feel sure Mark wouldn't have minded! As I sat in the gallery watching Nicholas recreating the Brig (as everyone calls the character) I mused on the prospect of pairing the Brigadier with Doctor Number Two, Patrick Troughton – a reunion, as it were. Michael Glynn, the producer of *Emmerdale Farm* and a former colleague on a BBC series I worked on in the early seventies called *The Venturers*, had telephoned me earlier that day to say that Frazer Hines could not be freed from his commitments to the Yorkshire soap-opera. However Michael, much nearer our shooting date, did graciously allow Frazer a couple of days off in order to appear briefly as a spectre in the programme.

There was more than a touch of Laurel and Hardy about the reunion of the Brig and Doctor Number Two, aided undoubtedly by the wit of the two actors, both of whom have an astute sense of humour.

I am often asked if there are any plans for the Brigadier to return to the series to accompany the latest incarnation of the Doctor, Nicholas having worked in the series with all other five Doctors, and my answer is, undoubtedly! When the right script turns up!

11

DODO

Played by Jackie Lane
First Appearance: *The Massacre*　26th February 1966
Last Appearance: *The War Machines*　2nd July 1966

One of the few companions during the series I have never actually met, although Jackie runs the 'voice-over' department of London Management (which represents among others Tom Baker). We have spoken to each other many times over the telephone.

HARRY SULLIVAN

Played by Ian Marter
First Appearance: *Robot*　28th December 1974
Last Appearance: *The Android Invasion*　13th December 1975

A character I liked enormously and wanted to bring back. Perhaps the author of the most memorable adaptations of the series's novelisations.

IAN CHESTERTON
Played by William Russell
First Appearance: *An Unearthly Child*   23rd November 1963
Last Appearance: *The Chase*   26th June 1965

An actor I have always admired since the successful series *Ivanhoe*.

JAMIE McCRIMMON
Played by Frazer Hines
First Appearance: *The Highlanders*   17th December 1966
Last Appearance: *The Two Doctors*   2nd March 1985

It seems extraordinary that twenty years ago this year Frazer Hines joined the Tardis crew. It seems particularly hard to believe because Frazer has hardly aged at all. Those of you who saw his brief return to *Doctor Who* in *The Five Doctors* three years ago and more recently in *The Two Doctors* will no doubt have noticed this.

The original script of *The Two Doctors* was set in New Orleans but due to a problem with our potential co-producers, filming became impossible there. The script was rewritten for Spain and more specifically Seville.

Anyone thinking that foreign filming is a free holiday for the cast and crew, who laze by the pool all day, couldn't be more wrong. The working day is usually fourteen hours long and the temperature in Seville was 115°F. I can recall many times watching Frazer prepare for a take by waving his kilt in order to cool down.

As many of you will know, Frazer is extremely quick-witted and has an endless array of the world's most corny jokes forever at the tip of his tongue. Many times during our filming in Seville, when tempers were beginning to fray, mainly due to the extreme heat, Frazer would come to the rescue with some appalling joke or other.

During *The Two Doctors*, Patrick Troughton spent some of the story confined to a wheelchair. Frazer and Colin Baker continually crept up behind Patrick's chair and shoved it as hard as they could whenever Patrick was taking a nap! Great fun but not to be imitated with infirm relatives.

JO GRANT

Played by Katy Manning
First Appearance: *The Terror of the Autons*   2nd January 1971
Last Appearance: *The Green Death*   23rd June 1973

Katy now lives in Australia.

K9

Voices of John Leeson and David Brierley
First Appearance: *The Invisible Enemy*   1st October 1977
Last Appearance: *The Five Doctors*   25th November 1983

K9, the Doctor's mobile computer, was devised by writers Bob Baker and Dave Martin, originally for the story *The Invisible Enemy* only. Graham Williams, the then producer, asked script editor Robert Holmes and myself (I was then production unit manager) what we thought of the metal mutt itself, which had been so brilliantly designed by Tony Harding. Robert and I both thought it was stunning and said so. 'Good,' said Graham, 'I want to keep it as a regular companion.' In many ways, Graham's decision then appeared to be imitated throughout the world in both films and television, as every sci-fi project hurriedly introduced a 'cutesy-robot'. But to my knowledge, K9 was the first, and in conceptual terms the best.

There were endless problems, however. The radio-control signal interfered with the television cameras in the studio. Hardboard paths had to be used on location to provide the necessary flat surface for K9 to run on – expensive tank-tracks which were added to facilitate easier movement on bumpy surfaces just didn't work. I even remember Tom Baker saying that the dog couldn't even traverse a piece of Sellotape without faltering. Nevertheless, Graham's gamble paid off and K9 became one of the most popular additions to *Doctor Who*.

When I took over as producer for the eighteenth series, John Leeson had decided not to continue as the voice of K9 and David Brierley had replaced him. With all due respect to David, who is a fine actor, I felt that K9 lacked the sparkle that John Leeson had injected into the characterisation. What's more, I decided the moment I took over at the helm of the show, that K9 should go. Just as Graham's decision to bring in the dog was a first, so Doctor Who should lead the way in being the first to dispense with the artefact and make way for other newer ideas.

In any case, K9 was rather too clever for its own good, and writers were using it as an easy way out of cliff-hanger situations. 'K9 to the rescue!' was becoming a bit of a bore.

So I planned that K9 would leave with Romana twenty episodes into the eighteenth season.

I wondered too if John Leeson would rejoin the show if there were a set number of episodes, as his main reason for leaving was an apparently open-ended contract for the voice. I was absolutely delighted when he agreed to return, and K9 regained its former sparkle.

It was because of the outcry when we announced K9's departure that I saw the potential of K9 having its own series. Whilst I didn't think it was right

for *Doctor Who* any longer, I thought that it could well succeed in the right vehicle. And so Christopher and I devised a series originally entitled *A Girl's Best Friend*, later to become known as *K9 and Company* (*A Girl's Best Friend* was retained as the story title).

We hoped that this one-off Christmas special would develop into a series, but unfortunately this was not to be.

I still think there is a place for K9 in a series such as *K9 and Company*. There's life in the old dog yet!

K9

The Doctor has also engaged the assistance of K9 – his own real-time data analyser robot, which is in the form of a mechanical dog.
The current K9 is Mark II (Mark I was left on Gallifrey with Leela).
Unless K9 is immobilised, his eyes are always on and the panel on his back shows flashing lights. Around his neck is a dog collar with dog-tag attached.
When K9 is asked to consult his data banks, analyse objects, etc, his ears (or 'crisps') waggle.
From K9's mouth comes a ticker-tape, used, for example, when K9 is left alone to do a detailed analysis of a planet or whatever. The ticker-tape will no longer discharge on cue.
Set into K9's head between his eyes is a probe. This will extend to enable K9 to reach areas out of his immediate range (e.g. the under-surface of the Tardis central console).
In K9's snout area there is a blaster which will extend on cue. The blaster can kill or stun – the red ray from the blaster is achieved during the Gallery Only *session.*
K9's head can move up and down in order to direct his blaster towards a particular area or person. In the past K9's blaster ray has appeared to emanate at any required angle. In future please position the dog and his head to avoid this anomaly.
K9's tail can move up and down and from side to side.
The voice of K9 is John Leeson (engaged by producer).
The operator of K9 is Nigel Brackley.
There is a duplicate light-weight non-practical version of K9, in case any actor should have to carry K9 and be unable to manage the real model.

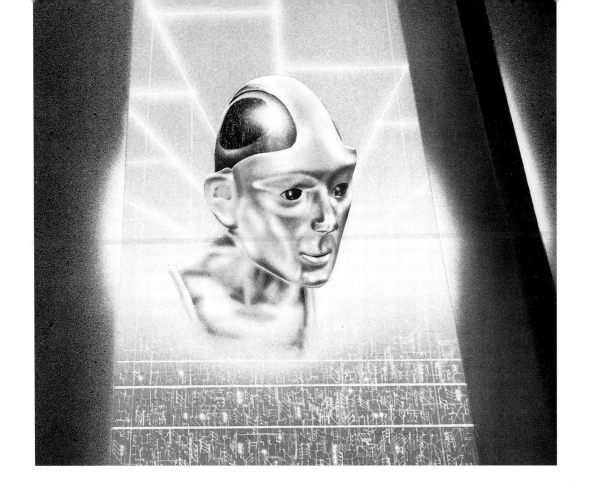

KAMELION

Voice of Gerald Flood
First Appearance: *The King's Demons*   16th March 1983
Last Appearance: *Planet of Fire*   2nd March 1984

Kamelion was an excellent idea for a companion – which didn't live up to expectations. The concept of a robot companion which could change its appearance at the whim of the person it regarded as its master, was an appealing one, but sadly its presence in the Tardis was short-lived.

It was while we were recording the first section of *Earthshock* that representative Richard Gregory and his partner, Chris Padmore of the Imagineering Company, first approached me with regard to a robot they possessed. Apparently, a feature movie had commissioned the robot, which moved its limbs, eyes, mouth etc. synchronously with a pre-recorded tape fitted into its back. For some reason the feature film had not come to fruition and the boys had the robot left on their shelf, and wondered if I could write it into *Doctor Who*.

From what I was told, I became intrigued and suggested they bring the robot to our next recording session of *Earthshock* (for which Imagineering supplied, amongst other things, the new-look Cybermen) and demonstrated it to me.

It was an extremely odd sight, two weeks later, to view a robot clad in just a pair of Speedo swim-trunks, talking and moving its head and body in the technical store of the studio. Despite its odd look, moving in time to some classical music, it was intriguing, and so I decided to use it.

A few weeks later Eric Saward, myself and Terence Dudley, who was to write its debut story, travelled to the Imagineering workshop in Oxfordshire to view the robot together. Terry invented the name Kamelion and it was his idea that Kamelion should change at its master's request.

The chief problem with Kamelion was the amount of programming time required to achieve synchronous movement with the recorded speech. It usually took eight or nine days to programme the 'beast' as we christened it. This meant that after the first read-through of a story, Gerald Flood, who provided Kamelion's voice as well as playing King John in the robot's debut story, had to rush off to the sound studio to record all Kamelion's dialogue, leaving space on the tape for interjections from the other actors in *all* its scenes. Inevitably, when we arrived at the studio, the pace of various scenes had changed and we discovered on occasions that Kamelion was talking at the same time as other actors. Sometimes there would be long pauses in the scene, depending on which way the pace had developed during rehearsal. All the scenes involving Kamelion were extremely difficult to record and there were several major breakdowns of the robot. We did not finish our taping and we had to remount this production. So it will not surprise you to learn that just as soon as Kamelion had joined the Doctor, the decision was taken to get rid of it.

The following season was to see its departure in the story *Planet of Fire* and I decided to include the 'beast' in only one other story that season prior to its departure, to remind our audience it existed. Consequently, a scene was recorded featuring Kamelion, Tegan and the Doctor for the first episode of *The Awakening*. However, when this episode was edited, it was drastically over-length. We were unable to persuade the planning

department to give us extra transmission time, so we made some cuts and one of the first scenes to go was the one with Kamelion. As it happened it was a good scene, and Kamelion behaved well on recording, but as mentioned earlier, the scene had no plot relevance to the story – it was simply included as a reminder.

Thirdly and finally, *Planet of Fire* saw the demise of Kamelion. We deliberately kept its contribution relatively minor in this story for practical reasons. Those of you who have seen the story will remember that a half-human Kamelion was introduced (played in silver paint by Dallas Adams) to avoid taking three more people onto location. Also, we had a feeling that the Spanish authorities might have been alarmed by the 'beast's' arrival in the customs hall at Lanzarote airport.

I have no regrets about trying what we did. Kamelion was a brilliant concept of the Imagineering Company, and if only we had had more time (a constant plea of producers) Kamelion would have featured much more often and had a much longer stay with the Doctor.

KATARINA

Played by Adrienne Hill
First Appearance: *The Myth Makers*   6th November 1965
Last Appearance: *The Dalek Masterplan*   29th January 1967

Adrienne, who has resisted long term association with *Doctor Who*, joined the team as part of the BBC's *Children in Need* appeal in 1985.

LEELA

Played by Louise Jameson
First Appearance: *The Face of Evil*   1st January 1977
Last Appearance: *The Invasion of Time*   11th March 1978

I adored Leela! She was a marvellous character and complemented the Doctor perfectly. Her tendency to stumble into trouble like a bull in a china shop endeared her to me and to the general public like no other companion before. A savage whose solution to every problem was to withdraw her knife from its sheath, gave the Doctor a chance to demonstrate more readily the paternalistic nature of the role.

I was part of the team that worked on Louise's last six stories and I'm always delighted to see Louise at conventions here and abroad.

LIZ SHAW

Played by Caroline John
First Appearance: *Spearhead from Space*   3rd January 1970
Last Appearance: *The Five Doctors*   25th November 1983

The first time I worked with Caroline John was on the story *The Ambassadors of Death* in 1970. She is married to actor Geoffrey Beevers who played The Master in the story *Keeper of Traken*.

THE MASTER

Played by Roger Delgado, Peter Pratt,
Geoffrey Beevers, Anthony Ainley
First Appearance: *The Terror of the Autons*   2nd January 1971
Latest Re-appearance: *The Mark of the Rani*   9th February 1982

I make no excuses at all for including The Master in a book about companions. Of course, this chapter shouldn't be here at all, but the character is so much a part of *Doctor Who* mythology, that I felt I wanted to include him.

As a floor assistant in the drama serials department, my first encounter with The Master was with the original incarnation, the late great Roger Delgado in the story *Colony in Space* in 1971. Much has been said and written about Roger and his delightful personality and I feel compelled to echo the opinions of all those who ever worked with him. He was a totally professional, highly intelligent and completely charming gentleman. A gentle man and a gentleman. His tragic death means the profession is the poorer. I never worked with the late Peter Pratt, but I remember watching the story *The Deadly Assassin* in 1976 when under Philip Hinchcliffe's guidance The Master was re-introduced to *Doctor Who*. I was chilled by

his portrayal and delighted that the Doctor's arch-enemy had been brought back.

When the original script of *The Keeper of Traken* was delivered there was no Master included in it. It was while Christopher and I were discussing changes to be incorporated in the script that I came up with the idea of the statue Melkur representing something, and subsequently that the statue in fact should be The Master's Tardis, or rather one of them.

It was John Black who came up with the idea of casting Geoffrey Beevers as the decrepit Master and a good choice it was too. At that time I was occupied with thoughts of who should play the 'regenerated' Master and Tremas, the character whose body the decaying Master would take over. This was the first of many anagrams: TREMAS = MASTER and because it was the first, the most successful.

23

I had worked as production assistant on a long-running series called *The Pallisers* in 1973 in which Anthony Ainley played a revolting character called Reverend Emilius and it was this portrayal that resulted in my offering the role of The Master to 'Ant' as his friends call him.

It is extremely difficult for an actor to take over someone else's role, particularly when Roger Delgado had made the part so successfully his own. Peter Pratt and Geoffrey Beevers had had much easier times playing the part, in that their versions were The Master 'in decay' and they were shrouded in cowls and covered in make-up. But now Anthony had to pay tribute to a fully-fledged creation of a part and at the same time make it his own. Naturally we did not want a carbon copy of what had gone before. If we had, maybe we would have asked Mike Yarwood to play the part. The beard and moustache were essential, in my view, as was a predominance of black in the costume.

It was astounding to us all, therefore, when late at night in the studio, attempting the very tricky effort of the decaying Master taking over Tremas's body and emerging as the new Master, we noticed the staggering similarity to Roger Delgado.

I have re-used the character of The Master in every season I have produced. Some would argue this is too regular a use, but as I said at the beginning I make no excuses for including this marvellous character, devised by Barry Letts and Terrance Dicks.

NYSSA OF TRAKEN

Played by Sarah Sutton
First Appearance: *The Keeper of Traken*   31st January 1981
Last Re-appearance: *The Caves of Androzani*   16th March 1984

When writer Johnny Byrne created the role of Nyssa for the story *The Keeper of Traken* he had no idea that the character would become a regular companion. Nor did anyone else for that matter.

Nyssa's inclusion in the companion line-up was entirely due to Tom Baker's departure. Tom was and still is the actor who has played the

24

Doctor for the longest period of time – seven years. I felt it essential that we aid the transition from the longest-serving Doctor to Doctor Number Five with as many familiar companion faces as we could handle. Adric had already been introduced and we were committed to the introduction of Tegan. It seemed to me that Nyssa would make a highly useful adjunct to these two characters. So, when Sarah Sutton was auditioned by John Black, the director of *The Keeper of Traken*, I attended also. Sarah was engaged initially for *Traken* only, with an option on her services for more episodes, to be taken up if we were happy. At the supper break of Sarah's first recording day, I told her I was delighted with her performance and that she was to become a regular in *Doctor Who*. She was thrilled.

Because the original script contained a very brief description of Nyssa's character, Christopher H. Bidmead and I embroidered the breakdown, with the writer's permission of course, as follows:

Nyssa of Traken

Nyssa is the daughter of Tremas, first scientist and Consul of the Empire of Traken. Tremas is now dead at the hand of The Master, who has commandeered his cadaver by way of a thirteenth regeneration.

She is eighteen, of noble birth; an attractive young girl with values and skills deeply rooted in her Traken past. Tutored by her father in the advanced sciences, she is already a skilled apprentice in bioelectronics, a discipline in which her people excelled.

Nyssa is an open young woman. Idealistic and pragmatic by turn, she has an abiding belief in the essential goodness of all things, which sometimes blinds her to the less overt manifestations of evil. For example, in meeting The Master for the first time in his new guise she has mistaken him for her father, only being rescued from his clutches by the intervention of Adric and the Doctor. A threat once visible, however, brings out all that is best in Nyssa: calm assessment, lightning judgement, and nicely-judged action.

Nyssa's aristocratic background sometimes leaves her oblivious to the simpler needs of others, and occasionally prevents her from seeing the funny side of situations. Adric, an orphan like her, is very fond of Nyssa, but at times her innocence, seriousness and inability to compromise seem to him like deliberate stubbornness.

The Doctor feels, irrationally, a sense of responsibility for the death of her father, but has too much respect for her individuality to see himself as any

25

kind of substitute. He appears, in his off-hand way, to enjoy having her around and being in some small part a force in her spiritual development. He would never allow it to be seen that deep, deep down inside, the presence of all these young people in the Tardis is very wearing!

The name Nyssa was devised by Johnny Byrne and consequently he has retained copyright in the character. Each time Nyssa appeared, Johnny received an appropriate fee. This is true of all characters in *Doctor Who* devised by individual writers and indeed in all TV productions.

Nyssa's costume initially fitted in perfectly with the settings and style of *Keepers of Traken*. However, the minute Nyssa's 'fairy frock', as it became known, was seen in another environment, it looked bizarre, and at times totally ridiculous. So, during the first story of the following series (Nyssa's third story) she changed the fairy skirt for a pair of figure-hugging pants which matched the original *Traken* bodice. And then the complaints started. I discovered that Nyssa's male following was rather older than I suspected, or certainly more precocious. From all over the country, letters poured in demanding a return sighting of Miss Sutton's legs. However, it was a year later before we changed the costume again.

It is worth pointing out that the maturing of a young actress does result in different styles of dress becoming necessary. As Sarah and many of the other female companions grew more mature, so they 'grew out' of the look of their costumes. In addition, it is impossible for current fashion trends to be ignored by costume designers, and quite rightly too. For example, Tegan's slightly futuristic air-hostess uniform first seen in early 1981 looks remarkably old-fashioned viewed five years later.

One of the scripts we were determined to use in the nineteenth season was called *Kinda* by a marvellous writer called Christopher Bailey. This had been commissioned with the brief to include two companions, Adric and Tegan. Needless to say, the script was in the pipeline before Nyssa joined the Tardis crew. On its delivery and following lengthy discussions with the author, none of us could come up with a satisfactory way of including Nyssa in the whole story without totally ruining its structure. So, Nyssa became ill at the beginning of episode one and recovered at the end of episode four, which justified her absence from the main storyline.

27

Sarah's favourite story during her stay as Nyssa was *Black Orchid*, a 1920s whodunnit. Sarah played a dual role, of which there have been many during my era of *Doctor Who* and I felt made a nice distinction between her portrayal of Nyssa and her 'double' Ann.

Nyssa was Peter Davison's favourite companion; he felt his Doctor worked best with Nyssa's innocence and idealism at his side. Whilst I don't totally agree with his choice, I must admit a great fondness for her. I too shed a tear during Nyssa's emotional farewell to the Doctor in the story *Terminus*. What more fitting exit for this aristocratic young lady than to devote her skills and her life to helping those less fortunate than herself.

PERPUGILLIAM BROWN

Played by Nicola Bryant
First Appearance: *Planet of Fire*   2nd March 1984
Last Appearance: Story yet untitled   Autumn 1986

Peri

Perpugilliam (Peri for short) Brown is a wealthy 18-year-old American student studying Botany. She has long blonde hair which complements her attractive looks. She does not suffer fools gladly and her most charming attribute is an acute sense of humour.
We meet Peri for the first time, while she is on holiday in whichever country we decide to film next season's foreign story.
Peri's mother, Janine, has remarried a man Peri dislikes – Howard. Peri still treasures the memory of her father who died when Peri was 13, particularly as her mother appears to care more for Howard's three children than for Peri herself. It is because of her respect for her father that Peri thinks so highly of the Doctor – to some extent the Doctor replaces the gap in Peri's life. When he died he was of the same age as the Doctor appears now. This never develops further than admiration and close friendship.
Peri is the kind of girl who is popular — not just because of her looks, but because her warmth and sense of fun make her appeal to people of all ages.

Originally, I did not intend Peri to be introduced in the same story where Turlough was to leave. The character was devised in February 1983 and it was not until May of that year that Peter Davison decided to make the

twenty-first season his last. Because of this decision Eric Saward and I had to rethink the season. I wanted the new Doctor to appear in at least one whole story, Tegan had to leave, we had to dispense with Kamelion for the practical reasons already discussed, Turlough was to leave, Peri was to join and the fifth Doctor was to regenerate. There were an awful lot of important comings and goings to be undertaken in twenty-six episodes.

After much thought we decided to ask Peter Grimwade to devise a story for us which introduced Peri, eliminated Kamelion and said farewell to Turlough. We also required the use of Lanzarote as a foreign planet and as itself, and as if that wasn't enough, to make what was to become *Planet of Fire* a Master story as well.

As you may remember, Peter wrote the story that introduced Turlough – *Mawdryn Undead*. At that time we told him to leave Turlough's origins a mystery, as some other writer would be required to explain all about the character in due course. How ironic then that this task should fall to Mr Grimwade himself. Nevertheless Peter, as always totally professional, tackled the formidable task and produced a script that cleverly didn't appear too bogged down with the all-important sub-plot.

The decision to try one solitary companion with the Doctor was an attempt to echo the Pertwee–Jo relationship of the seventies, which had been so successful, and it was therefore a great pity that we were unable to develop the Davison–Peri relationship more fully, due to Peter's impending departure.

Many people have speculated that the introduction of Peri was and is an attempt to pander to the American market. Let us dispel this myth once and for all. It is the very British-ness of the show that is enjoyed by our US cousins. If anything, an American companion is likely to displease rather than please them.

I have always felt it so implausible that the Doctor had so many Earth–UK companions. It is worth mentioning here too, that although there are distinct advantages in having alien companions, it is the Earth companion that our younger viewers find it easier to relate to, and our younger viewers must be considered!

Tegan was an enormously successful companion, some of this no doubt due to her being Australian, and so after Australia, why not the United States of America? The decision was an attempt to redress the balance of an Earth–UK companion-dominated programme. As you now know, the next companion is to be Earth–UK (much more feasible now that some 'foreigners' have been aboard the Tardis in recent years).

Much has been written about Peri's costumes. Miss Bryant herself has been quoted as saying she hates the costumes she is forced to wear.

At Nicola's launch, she wore her own clothes – a pair of shorts and a leotard top. I thought she looked so stunning that I asked our costume designers to echo Nicola's own clothes! Obviously we couldn't ask Nicola to wear skimpy shorts for our winter shoot on *Revelation of the Daleks* (it snowed heavily too) and so for the previous story we introduced an outfit dominated by trousers.

Elizabeth Rowell, a vastly experienced make-up designer, was given the responsibility of creating the Peri look. Nicola is so beautiful and has such excellent skin, that I wanted her to look relatively un-made-up. Just sufficient make-up to satisfy the intensity of light in the studios was all that was required. Nicola's hair was a different matter. When she auditioned for the part it was very long, falling right to her shoulders. This length hair is always a problem on camera. If the artist turns profile, quite often all you can see is hair. In order to avoid directors having to constantly readjust the camera position, I proposed that we should change the style of her tresses. Nicola, Liz Rowell and I spent a highly amusing morning with dozens of BBC wigs trying out the styles that would suit Nicola and Peri. In the end, we chose a style used by Wendy Padbury during the Troughton era.

Early in 1985, when the postponement of *Doctor Who* occurred, I had hoped to break the news to Nicola myself. However, I tried to telephone her several times one morning but was unable to get through to Nicola's home. In desperation, I called her agent and asked him to break the news for me. In the meantime, a reporter from the *Daily Mirror* who had had a tip-off, got through to Nicola to ask how she felt about 'the death of Doctor Who'. Nicola hung up, assuming that some awful accident had occurred to Colin Baker. So in one way she was relieved to hear from her agent that it was the show that was being rested.

Peri's first story with the sixth Doctor was an eventful one. What we intended and achieved was a very simple story in which the new Doctor demonstrated his new persona. It was deliberately structured so that by the end of the first episode of *The Twin Dilemma* the audience hated the new Doctor. Much of this was achieved by the Doctor's monstrous treatment of Peri. All credit must go to Colin's portrayal of course, for his venom, but perhaps equally to Nicola's Peri who suffered at his hands (he deliberately tried to strangle her) and who echoed the audience's lack of comprehension of what was going on in the mind of our hero.

Naturally, our objectives achieved for the first episode, we then spent three episodes with the audience and Peri gradually warming to the new character. Yet again the companion's role had been vital to the overall plan of campaign in carrying our audience into a new era of *Doctor Who*.

At the time of writing, we are about to embark on the delayed twenty-third season of the programme. Peri will leave the series during the season. She has been successful, without a doubt, but it is time to move on. *Doctor Who*'s development must continue.

POLLY

Played by Anneke Wills

First Appearance: *The War Machines*   25th June 1966
Last Appearance: *The Faceless Ones*   13th May 1967

Polly accompanied Ben throughout her stay in the Tardis.

ROMANA 1

Played by Mary Tamm

First Appearance: *The Ribos Operation*   2nd September 1978
Last Appearance: *The Armageddon Factor*   24th February 1979

Romana 1

Romana (dvratrelundar) originally joined the Doctor to assist in his quest for the Key to Time. *She was allocated to him by a Guardian of Time (White Guardian), initially against the Doctor's own will and better judgement.*

Romana is an acolyte Time Lord – yet to graduate from the Time Lords' Academy on Gallifrey – her studies being interrupted by her present assignment to the Doctor.

The Doctor is sometimes surprised, and even annoyed, at Romana's knowledge of later techniques than were available to him during his *undergraduate years. Romana also has two hearts. At the latest count, Romana is 125.*

The intelligence of Romana was substantial. However, in some ways this meant the character was at a distinct disadvantage from the start. The Doctor is a hugely intelligent alien, K9 was a sophisticated mobile computer and Romana an acolyte Time-Lady. This array of characters possessed such wide-reaching and all-encompassing knowledge and intelligence, we felt the 'baddies' of the stories were complete idiots, or at least they should pack up and run, the minute the Tardis crew reveal themselves.

In fairness, though, initially Romana was a fascinating character and her relationship with the Doctor interesting. I know that Mary Tamm, next to Bonnie Langford the most well-known companion *prior* to joining *Doctor Who*, was excited at the character's possibilities. However, as I mentioned in the introduction, character development in the companions tends to be rather slow, as it often gets in the way of the drama and after all, the show is called *Doctor Who*. Apparently as the sixteenth season developed, Mary was concerned that her character didn't progress. In some ways she felt it regressed. I have no doubt that this partly affected her decision not to stay after twenty-six episodes.

It was director George Spenton-Foster who suggested to producer Graham Williams that Mary should play Romana. I remember well the screen test that took place in one of the BBC's presentation studios at TV Centre. George, Graham, myself and script editor Anthony Read, watched from the gallery while the last four candidates for the part played a scripted scene with Tom Baker. All the actresses were dressed in white, as Romana was to make her first appearance in an amazing white creation designed by June Hudson. Mary was a popular choice and she proved popular with the public, despite the difficulties created by the character.

ROMANA 2

Played by Lalla Ward
First Appearance: *Destiny of the Daleks*   1st September 1979
Last Appearance: *Warriors' Gate*   24th June 1981

When Lalla Ward took over the role of Romana, things changed – obviously a totally different actress playing the part brings something totally different to that part. Most importantly though, Romana's brightness was played down, and more vulnerability was introduced – a stock trait of *Doctor Who* companions. This vulnerability, naivety almost, was emphasised by the immature regeneration sequence, where Romana chose her new image rather like choosing a new dress.

Lalla selected most of her own costumes during the series, occasionally even designing them herself. She chose costumes that children, in her opinion, would be amused by: a pink copy of the Doctor's costume, a 1920s bathing outfit for the sequence on Brighton beach, a Little Lord Fauntleroy outfit for *Meglos* etc. The only one I didn't feel worked too well, perhaps because of its utter simplicity, was the Chinese peasant outfit which Lalla wore in her last story, *Warriors' Gate*.

There is a wine bar near my office called Albertine's (where *EastEnders* was devised – hence Albert Square) and Lalla and I meet there occasionally for a social lunch. Every single time this happens, other TV personnel assume she is returning to *Doctor Who*. No wonder rumours start flying around – it seems some of them are started by BBC staff themselves!

Lalla, of course, married her Doctor, Tom Baker. Graeme McDonald, the then head of series and serials department, and I went along to Chelsea Registry Office to wish the bride and groom well, scatter confetti and join in the celebration afterwards. Sadly, the marriage is no longer.

Following her stint in *Doctor Who*, Lalla did not work as an actress for a while. I know she felt she was suffering because of being well-known in a popular series. Type-casting, in my opinion, is something that companions in *Doctor Who* suffer more than the Doctors. Strange, when you consider there have been so many more companions than Doctors.

Fortunately, though, Lalla is talented in other areas and so book illustrating and book writing have kept her busy. Recently, the jinx of type-casting in *Doctor Who* was broken and she has just finished shooting a TV film programme called *Riviera*. I'm delighted this talented actress is beginning to get the work she so richly deserves.

SARA KINGDOM

Played by Jean Marsh
First and Last Appearances: *The Dalek Masterplan* Nov/Dec/Jan 1966/7

The shortest-running companion in *Doctor Who*'s history. She joined the Doctor and was killed in the same story – which to date is the longest *Doctor Who* story ever.

SARAH JANE SMITH

Played by Lis Sladen
First Appearance: *The Time Warrior*   15th December 1973
Last Re-appearance: *The Five Doctors*   15th November 1983

Sarah Jane Smith is probably the most popular companion in the history of *Doctor Who*. The impact of the role initially was partly due, no doubt, to the advent of women's lib. In addition to the regular attributes of companions in the series dealt with in the introduction, Sarah Jane was a much more rounded character: independent yet fiercely loyal, she spoke her mind and this, to some extent, made her extremely popular, though not always with the Doctor.

I had so enjoyed the role of Sarah and more especially the performance of Lis Sladen, that when I took over as producer, I attempted to lure Lis back to the show. My attempt failed but Lis refused in such a charming and rationalised way that I was determined to work with her at a later date.

I was not to wait long! *K9 and Company* had been accepted as a pilot programme, and I decided this was the opportunity I needed to work with Lis. But would Lis be prepared to play Sarah Jane Smith in what was, after all, a *Doctor Who* spin-off? The answer was yes. And the reason? Well, as I explained at the time, this was most definitely an opportunity for both Sarah and Lis to excel. In *Doctor Who* Sarah was the Doctor's companion, in *K9 and Company* Sarah was, in effect, the Doctor. Sarah was the leading lady of the show and she was to take all the initiative. I promised to introduce a younger male character called Brendan to take over the place vacated by Sarah. Lis thoroughly enjoyed *K9 and Company* as did the entire team, and she was most disappointed at the decision not to make a complete series.

I'm sure it was because of *K9 and Company* that Lis was subsequently delighted to return to the main programme for *The Five Doctors*. Lis and Jon Pertwee had always worked well together and they were 'back in the old routine' in minutes, although the weather was ferociously cold and both were turning blue.

Lis is married to actor Brian Miller, who appeared in the *Doctor Who* story *Snakedance* and subsequently as the voice of a Dalek in *Resurrection of the Daleks*. They are a delightful couple and we don't see each other nearly enough. We only ever seem to be in each other's company in vast American hotels when we're doing conventions together. This seems a great pity to me!

STEVEN TAYLOR

Played by Peter Purves
First Appearance: *The Time Meddler*   3rd July 1965
Last Appearance: *The Savages*   18th June 1966

Peter Purves recently touched base with *Doctor Who* twice in two months. He joined us for the *Children in Need* appeal and then directed Colin Baker's pantomime *Aladdin* at Hayes in Middlesex.

When I first joined the BBC in December 1968, I worked with Peter for a short while on *Blue Peter*.

SUSAN FOREMAN

Played by Carole Ann Ford
First Appearance: *An Unearthly Child*   23rd November 1963
Last Appearance: *The Five Doctors*   25th November 1983

Doctor Who has been peppered with lovely ladies and Carole still looks absolutely gorgeous. I was delighted when she agreed to join us for our twentieth anniversary programme.

TEGAN JOVANKA

Played by Janet Fielding
First Appearance: *Logopolis*   28th February 1981
Last Appearance: *Resurrection of the Daleks*   15th February 1984

Tegan Jovanka

Tegan is twenty-one, an attractive and intelligent Australian trainee air stewardess, whose brash confidence in her own abilities actually conceals inner insecurity, a state of affairs that becomes clear in moments of stress.

On her way to her first real flight she accidentally blunders into the Tardis and thus finds herself being inadvertently abducted by the Doctor. Characteristically her inner bewilderment at the new situation in which she finds herself causes her to assume an attitude of overweening self-assertion, and she begins to take charge of the Doctor and Adric.

During the course of the stories, Tegan's superficial self-assurance will build until it becomes a real problem for the other occupants of the Tardis, and it will need drastic action on the part of the Doctor to put things to rights and show her the error of her ways.

The above is how Christopher H. Bidmead, script editor for the eighteenth season, and I envisaged Tegan.

The original description saw her as nineteen years old but at that time no air-hostesses were under twenty-one, so the document was amended. Also on the original there was one additional sentence. 'She may or may not continue with the Doctor after three stories.' I had decided originally to introduce Tegan for a trial period only. However, when Tom Baker decided to relinquish the role of the Doctor, I decided to 'pepper' the Tardis with companions, and although the requests for agents' suggestions for this part were distributed with a guarantee of only three stories, by the time I had found Tegan, the decision to make her a long-running companion had been made.

There is a minimum height requirement for air-hostesses and it is five feet four inches – my secretary had checked this with various airlines. So, when my office was deluged with suggestions for the part, I sifted through them on a height basis initially. Also, I had a particular groomed look in mind and a fairly good idea of the kind of face I was looking for. When Janet Fielding's photograph arrived, she looked totally wrong.

In addition, there was no mention of her height on her curriculum vitae supplied along with her photograph by the Actors Alliance, a group of actors acting as agents for each other. Nevertheless, the letter accompanying all this was highly amusing, and said that Janet Fielding was ideal for the part, as she *was* a terribly bossy Australian.

Although I thought she was totally wrong, I agreed to see her.

When she arrived I was immediately impressed by her self-confidence and sense of humour, but I noticed her distinct lack of height for the part. When I questioned her on this, she replied that she was five feet two inches, the minimum height for an air-hostess. I explained that it was, in fact, five feet four inches and she went into a lengthy explanation about Qantas, Singapore and Malaysian Airlines all having a two-inch-less height requirement, mentioning the 'small' people of the Far East. 'This girl's done her homework,' I thought. Little did I know she was lying.

She told me she was almost twenty-one, and after several weeks of auditions, recalls, etc., I decided to cast Janet Fielding as Tegan. She was certainly the most impressive of all the actresses interviewed.

A year later I had to apply to the Home Office for a permit to extend Janet's working visa in order for her to continue playing the part. It was simply a matter of my signing a document, stating I guaranteed her employment for the coming twelve months. I did notice that the form had been completed in pencil, but thought no more about it. A week later the document was returned to me, as her employer, stamped and approved by the Home Office and filled out in ink. Imagine my surprise to discover her age was three years older than I expected!

I sent the document with a brief note that said, 'I note your age with interest' to the rehearsal room at North Acton. I was due to see my run-through of the current show two days later. I was to get my revenge. Janet spent two days showing the note to everyone in the cast, convinced she was going to get the sack!

After Janet's initial contract had been drawn up and signed, the question of costume and make-up arose. I had asked Dorka Nieradzik, our highly talented make-up designer, to come up with a 'Tegan' haircut. Her design was splendid and I had high hopes of our popularising this particular cut, rather like Princess Diana did with her own captivating style. However, the hair salon in London's West End which we went to in order to realise Dorka's design, did not do the design justice and in fact, made a hash of the whole thing. Dorka had to partially re-style it back at the BBC.

On the costume front, June Hudson, another talented lady, designed Tegan's air-hostess uniform with which both Janet and I were delighted. However, even with that there was a problem. Janet was adamant that she should wear boots! I was appalled! I just couldn't understand Janet's reasons for covering her legs. Eventually it was revealed that a particularly ungallant 'gentleman' had told her that she had dreadful legs. (This explained the calf-length skirt and boots she wore at her first photocall,

41

about which I had been none too pleased.) Nevertheless, with a combination of 'pulling rank' and genuine flattery with regard to the lady's legs, a pair of heeled court shoes was chosen.

Tegan's first story was *Logopolis*, and considering this was her television debut, she made an impressive start. She was to settle down over the following seasons and in two particular stories, *Kinda* and *Snakedance*, was to deliver her best performances.

When Christopher Bidmead and I started with our blank sheet of paper to devise a new companion, little did we realise how popular Tegan would become. Originally, I had made a few notes about the character, which I asked Chris to embroider. I couldn't decide on a name at first – it was to be either Tegan (a friend's niece in Sydney, Australia is called Tegan), or Jovanka (the name of President Tito's widow), and at the top of the paper I had written 'Tegan – Jovanka'. Christopher assumed that Jovanka was her surname-to-be, rather than an alternative, and Tegan Jovanka was born.

During the twenty-first season came the time to say farewell to Tegan – we were about to embark on a new era of the show – with a new Doctor – and I decided to give Tegan a tear-jerking farewell. Many have criticised the way in which Tegan left, despairing at the death and destruction of the Doctor's world, but I felt and still feel totally convinced this was a valid and interesting development in the plucky, self-assured character's life.

TURLOUGH

Played by Mark Strickson
First Appearance: *Mawdryn Undead*   1st February 1983
Last Appearance: *Planet of Fire*   2nd March 1984

'What if the Doctor were given a companion who was up to no good?' So went one of the questions at a script conference with Eric Saward. Eric was enthusiastic, so Turlough was born. We decided that initially only the audience would be aware of Turlough's misdemeanours and shortcomings. This was to be followed by his fellow companions, most notably Tegan, being aware that all was not what it seemed in relation to the public school-boy from Brendan School. Finally, we were to reveal that the Doctor was no fool with regard to his quietly-observed feelings about Turlough and that the latter would finally choose good rather than evil when faced with the ultimate choice. There's only one thing wrong with all that – it was a little too cosy. 'Evil companion turned good' would reduce Turlough's character to being rather banal, and so it was agreed that even after Turlough had proved himself to be worthy of his position in the Tardis, there would be occasional glimpses of a large question mark looming over the character. Much more interesting, I'm sure you'll agree.

Turlough is one of my favourite companions in the show's history and I think it was chiefly his unpredictability that for me made him so. Often, as mentioned earlier, after an initially interesting character, mediocrity sets in in terms of development. With Turlough we had freedom, he had no set way of reacting because he had never fallen into the companion mould.

Much credit is due to Mark Strickson's portrayal of Turlough, but I nearly didn't get him.

When I was endlessly auditioning prospective 'Turloughs', I received a phone call from Mark's then agent Jan Evans telling me she was absolutely convinced Mark would be ideal.

On the arranged day of Mark's audition, Julia Smith, who was then producing *Angels*, came to see me, as she had a major problem. One of the leading actors in *Angels*, who was playing an ambulance driver, had fallen ill and had had to be removed from the production.

Mark had played his friend and co-driver in a few episodes some weeks before and Julia felt that with some rewriting, Mark could take over the storyline of the unwell actor on a long-term basis. Julia consequently said there was little point in my auditioning him as she was offering him a firm job. However, I insisted that I should proceed as planned. Mark was the last but one actor I saw for the part and by far the most splendid. I offered him the part later that afternoon, much to the chagrin of Julia! Mark couldn't believe it. Earlier that day he was out of work and by late afternoon that eventful Friday, he was being offered two years' work by two different producers. We gave Mark the weekend to think about it, as after all, ultimately it was his choice and I was delighted to hear on the following Monday that Mark had chosen *Doctor Who*. Apparently he had made his decision after being knocked off his bicycle by a lorry! I wonder who was driving the lorry!

I particularly liked the line-up of Tegan, Turlough and the Doctor – it seemed to me that the slightly sinister Turlough and the loud-mouthed Tegan created an interesting chemistry, out of which the fifth Doctor blossomed.

Mark was a wonderful company member, always smiling, charming and hard-working; also, in some ways a very gentle person, who regards his private life as just that. I am openly keen on all manner of publicity – it is an essential part of the process of making TV programmes. Publicity makes the public aware that a twenty-three-year-old show is still running, for example. Because of my keenness in this area, I remember Mark coming to see me to let me know that he was getting married to the lovely actress Julie Brennan and 'Please, John,' he said emotionally, 'no publicity!' His wishes were respected, of course.

VICKI

Played by Maureen O'Brien
First Appearance: *The Rescue*   2nd January 1965
Last Appearance: *The Myth Makers*   6th November 1965

Maureen, too, helped raise £4,000,000 for the BBC's annual *Children in Need* appeal. It was wonderful to welcome her back to the *Doctor Who* fold.

VICTORIA WATERFIELD

Played by Deborah Watling
First Appearance: *The Evil of the Daleks*   20th May 1967
Last Appearance: *Fury from the Deep*   20th April 1968

A little-known fact is that I invited Debbie to join us for *The Five Doctors*. Unfortunately, a major role in the *Dave Allen* series made this impossible.

ZOË

Played by Wendy Padbury
First Appearance: *The Wheel in Space*   27th April 1968
Last Appearance: *The Five Doctors*   25th November 1983

MELANIE

A new companion

The postponement of the twenty-third season of *Doctor Who* provided the team with something it had never had before to any great degree – TIME. A season of programmes usually takes slightly longer than a year to produce, so you will appreciate that normally the first director for a season arrives before the last story of the previous season is ready for transmission. However, following the announcement of the now 'notorious' delay, we were able to take stock of current trends, plan in a much more leisurely way than usual and discuss changes which could be made to improve the programme generally.

One of the changes we decided to make in preparation for what, at the moment, we consider 'next' season, is a change of emphasis in humour. I have always maintained that *Doctor Who* should have a helping of wit rather than slapstick. In order to make this helping more than ample I decided to devise a companion whose basic character gave the writers more opportunity for fun and humour; a character who, by her very nature, placed the Doctor and herself in humorous situations.

So it was in July 1985 that I sat down to devise the following:

Melanie

Melanie is scintillating, fascinating and irritating. She has a mane of red hair, fierce blue eyes and freckles. She is twenty-one years old and a computer programmer from Pease Potage, Sussex.
In 1986, when The Master attempted a massive computer fraud involving all the banking houses in the world, Melanie joined forces with the Doctor, helping to defeat The Master's dastardly plan, and has now been with him for some three months (in Earth time).

46

Melanie is one of those annoying young ladies who is a 'feminist' at all times, except at moments of great stress, when she relies heavily on playing the hard-done-by, down-trodden, crocodile-teared female.

She is heavily into aerobics and health food. She considers the Doctor overweight and in need of regular Jane Fonda-type movement lessons, although the Doctor insists he gets quite enough exercise dashing round the Galaxy, defeating evil. She often attempts to force health-giving vitamin-enriched food on the Doctor (muesli, raw carrots etc), which may provide useful comedy relief.

Despite her feminist attitudes, she appears to attempt to stabilise the Doctor's hitherto, in her opinion, unhealthy and irrational way of life.

She has a strong sense of humour and is often heard singing in the Tardis, much to the annoyance of the Doctor.

Although the Doctor is ferociously fond of Melanie, who prefers to be known as Mel (well, she would, wouldn't she?), he resists all attempts to stabilise his existence.

Melanie is the first Earth–UK companion for twelve years. We shall soon see why.

Mel screams well and runs down corridors with élan. (Despite being a computer programmer, Melanie cannot operate the Tardis. On the odd occasion that she tries, disaster ensues.)

When we got round to announcing the newest companion, Bonnie Langford, in January 1986, it was the most impressive *Doctor Who* press call to date.

As Bonnie was still appearing in *Peter Pan*, it was suggested by press officer, Kevin O'Shea, that we should make the announcement and subsequent photo-call from the stage of the Aldwych Theatre. I took this a stage further and suggested both Colin Baker and Bonnie were 'flown' by wires. Mark Furness, the management presenting *Peter Pan*, agreed to loan us the set and the wires.

Colin, of course, had used wires in *Doctor Who* before – *The Two Doctors*, *Time-Lash* etc, but when we arrived at the theatre for the photo-call, it was revealed that Colin had put on quite a bit of weight and none of the *Peter Pan* harnesses, which anchor the wires, was big enough! Hurriedly, a larger harness was collected from a nearby supplier and after one quick rehearsal, the Doctor and Melanie were up, up and away. Against a star backdrop, the resulting photographs were first class. However, most of the press seized on Colin's larger size combined with Melanie's decision to put the Doctor on a diet and made rather more of this in print than we envisaged. One newspaper even referred to *Doctor Huge*.

Ah well, *Doctor Who* is back in the news and back in production. The recent hiatus is over and we're set and raring to go with a new companion. All that's left to say is no matter who *your* favourite companion is to date, I trust you'll enjoy the new companion and most importantly, the new season.

WHO'S WHO

The list of illustrations is as follows: Adric, page 9, Brigadier, page 12, Jamie, page 15, K9, page 16, Kamelion, page 18, Leela, page 20, The Master, page 23, Nyssa, page 26, Peri, page 29, Romana 1, page 32, Romana 2, page 35, Sarah Jane, page 38, Tegan, page 41, Turlough, page 45.